My
ulf world
and me

Non-fiction Level
2

T0385824

What's the weather like today?

y **Kate Riddle**

WAYS LEARNING

PEARSON

What's the weather like today?
It's hot.

T-shirt

skirt

shorts

swimming shorts

When it's hot, I wear these clothes.

3

What's the weather like today?
It's sunny.

When it's sunny,
I wear my sunglasses and a hat.

What's the weather like today?
It's cold.

sweater

jacket

hat

scarf

When it's cold,
I wear these clothes.

7

What's the weather like today?
It's raining.

raincoat

When it's raining,
I wear a raincoat.

What's the weather like today?
It's windy.

When it's windy, sand sometimes
blows onto the road.

What's the weather like today?
It's foggy.

When it's foggy,
it is sometimes hard to see.

What's the weather like today?
It's stormy.

When it's stormy, the sky can get dark and sometimes there are sandstorms.

hot

sunny

cold

raining

windy

stormy

foggy